Can I Go?

Written by
Stephen Rickard

Rans⬤m

Can I go to the den?

No! I can not go to the den.

Can I go to the top of the hill?

No! I can not go to the top of the hill.

Can I go to the log hut?

No! I can not go to the log hut.

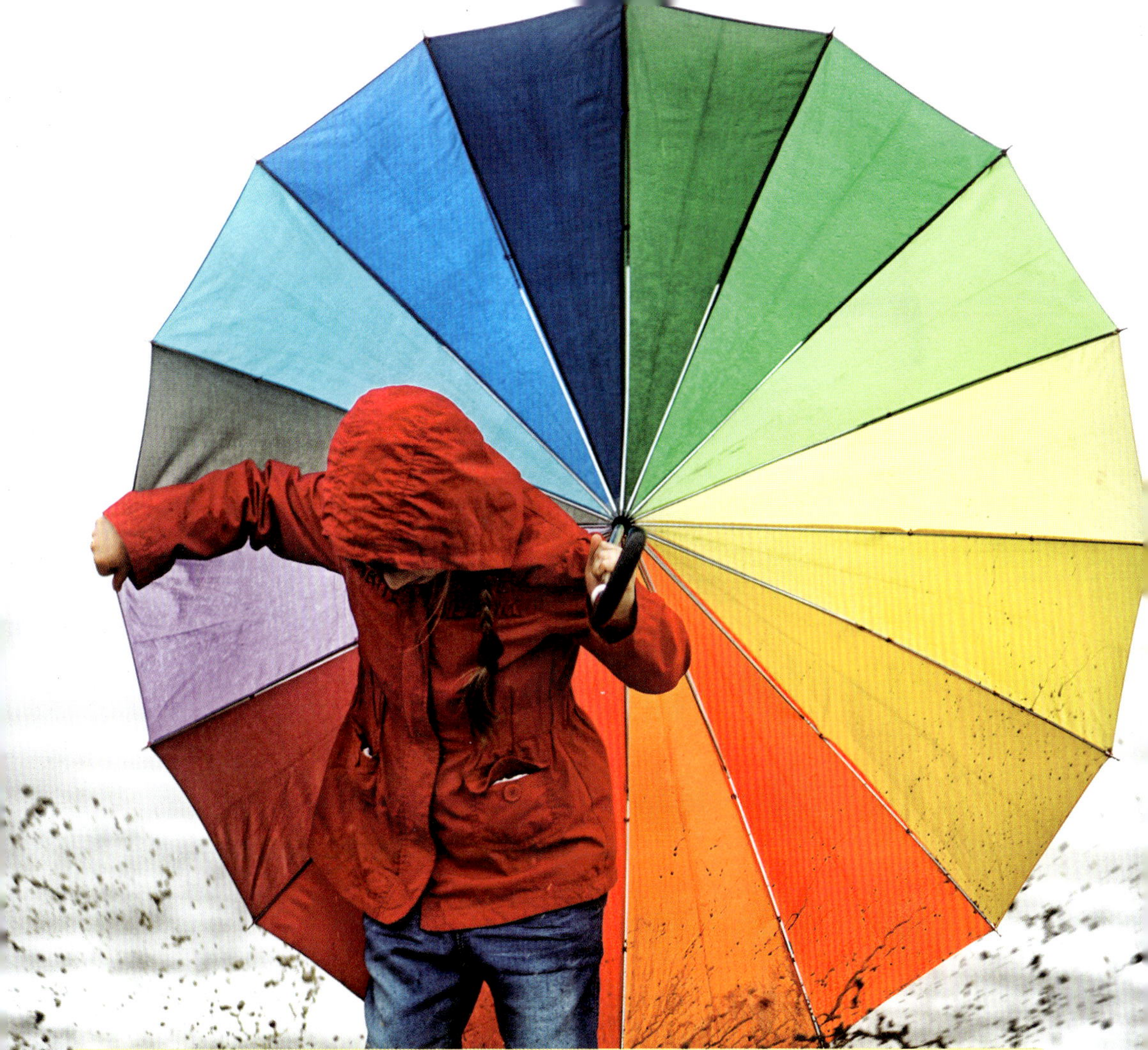

Can I go and run in the mud?

No! I can not go and run in the mud.

Can I go on the bus?

No! I can not go on the bus.

Can I run in the sun?

No! I can not run in the sun.

I can not go to the den
and I can not go to the top
of the hill.

I can not go to the log hut
and I can not go and run in
the mud.

I can not go on the bus and
I can not run in the sun.

I am in bed. I am ill!